FACING UNCERTAINTY

BY GOLRIZ GOLKAR

BLUE OWL
BOOKS

TIPS FOR CAREGIVERS

Social and emotional learning (SEL) helps children manage emotions, create and achieve goals, maintain relationships, learn how to feel empathy, and make good decisions. The SEL approach will help children establish positive habits in communication, cooperation, and decision-making. By incorporating SEL in early reading, children will be better equipped to build confidence and foster positive peer networks.

BEFORE READING

Talk to the reader about uncertainty. Explain how uncertainty can make a person feel anxious and afraid.

Discuss: Have you ever experienced uncertainty? How did it make you feel? Have you ever seen someone else experience uncertainty? How did you respond?

AFTER READING

Talk to the reader about managing uncertainty. Discuss ways to calm anxiety and fears when faced with uncertain situations.

Discuss: What can you do to calm down when faced with uncertainty? What can you do or say to help others when they feel uncertain?

SEL GOAL

Students who experience uncertainty may feel stressed and afraid. Help readers think of ways to manage their anxiety and fears. What kinds of self-care strategies can help them calm down? How can they help others cope with uncertainty?

TABLE OF CONTENTS

CHAPTER 1

WHAT IS UNCERTAINTY?

Emma is nervous for her first day at a new school. She doesn't know anyone, and she can't find her classroom. Ziggy and Nicole introduce themselves. They walk Emma to class. She feels calmer.

Emma was facing uncertainty. Uncertainty is being unsure about what will happen. You may feel **anxious**, scared, and upset. Your body may feel **tense**.

You may feel uncertain about experiencing something new. This could be getting braces or speaking in class. You may also feel uncertain when you are not sure when something will be **resolved**. Erin's dad lost his job. She feels uncertain because she's not sure when he will get another one.

Uncertainty can make it hard to sleep, eat, or **focus**. You may want to be left alone. But after you take time for yourself, it is important to ask for help and talk about your **emotions**.

CHAPTER 2

DEALING WITH UNCERTAINTY

Andy's grandpa is in the hospital. His mom tells him not to worry. But Andy is uncertain if his grandpa will get better. It makes him feel sad and anxious.

Andy draws a picture for his grandpa. It helps clear his head. After drawing, he feels calm. He hopes his grandpa will be OK.

When you feel uncertain, talk to a trusted adult. They can listen and help you feel better. Lola is afraid her parents will forget about her after her baby sister is born. She talks to her mom. Her mom **reassures** her they will always love her.

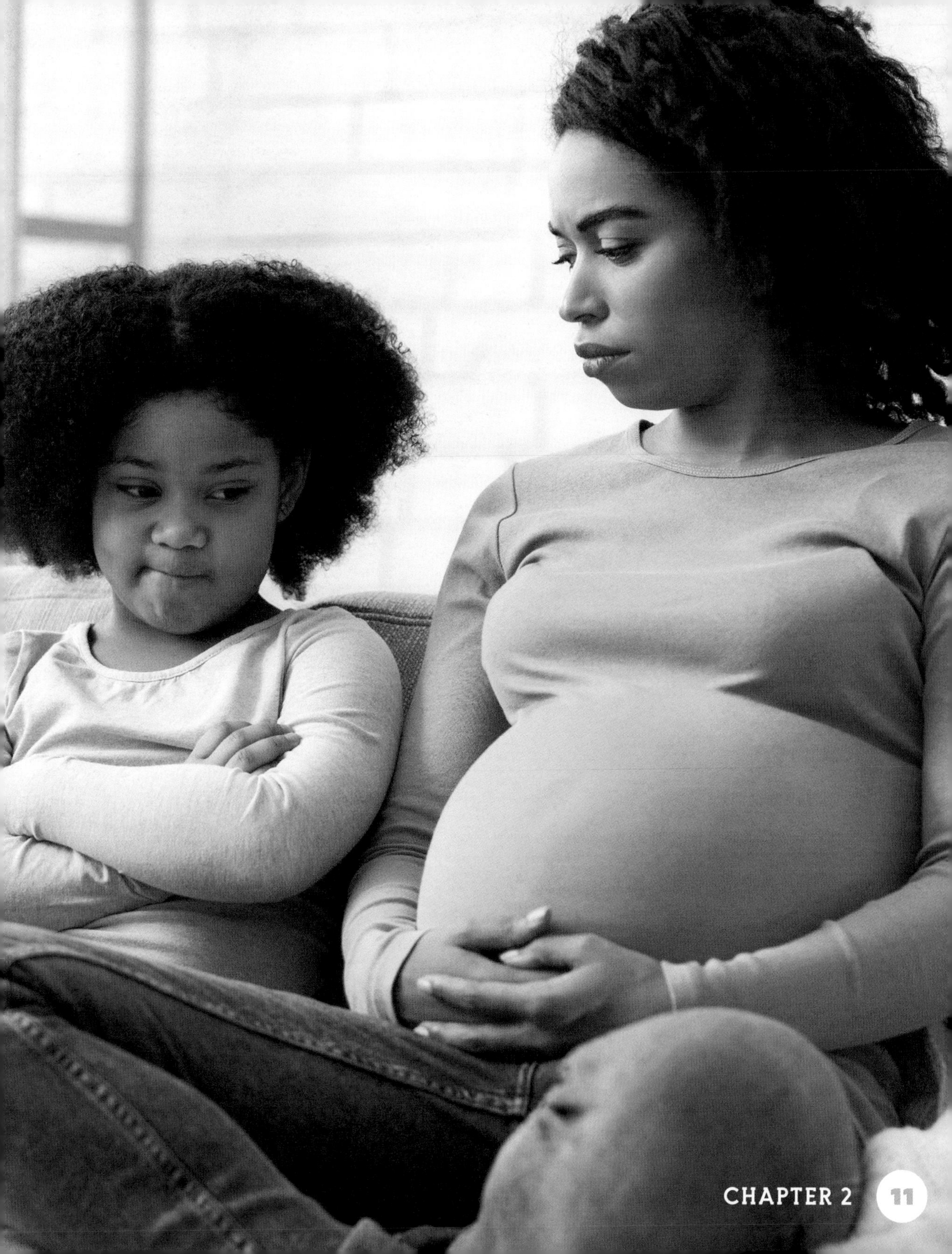

Cara feels uncertain about what others think of her. She often feels nervous in groups. This is **social anxiety**.

A group invites Cara to see a movie. But being in groups is hard for her. She asks her best friend Gina to join. She feels better going with a close friend.

FEELING SICK

Uncertainty may make you **panic**. You may feel dizzy or have stomach pains. If you feel sick, get help right away.

If you feel uncertain, learning to calm yourself can help. Stretch or exercise. This can ease anxiety. You can also **meditate**. Close your eyes and take deep breaths. Think of something that makes you happy.

FIND YOUR FUN

When you feel uncertain, do a favorite activity. You might paint, cook, or listen to music. Find what is fun for you. Fun activities can calm you.

CHAPTER 3

HELPING OTHERS

Help others who are facing uncertainty. Look out for people who seem nervous or alone. Ask them to join you and your friends.

Paul is nervous about a science test. Peter offers to help him study. Paul focuses better with Peter's help. They both do well on the test.

Maddie is uncertain if she will make the basketball team. Abby listens to her talk about her emotions. They go for a walk until Maddie feels better. Then they practice together.

Everyone deserves to be healthy and happy. **Support** others by talking to them. Help them think of ways to **cope**. Offer to exercise or play sports together. Breathe deeply and meditate with them. By helping one another, we can overcome uncertainty and feel better together.

STAYING HEALTHY

Staying healthy helps you cope with uncertainty. Exercise and eat healthy foods for **energy**. Sleep well to feel rested.

GOALS AND TOOLS

GROW WITH GOALS

Uncertainty can make you feel anxious and afraid.
Try these goals to help you cope with uncertainty.

Goal: Make a list of everything that makes you feel uncertain.
Think about why these things make you feel this way.

Goal: Make a list of activities and exercises you can practice
when you feel uncertain.

Goal: Think of ways to help others cope with uncertainty.
List some ways you can help others feel better.

TRY THIS!

Make a soothing box and a worry box to help you cope with uncertainty.

1. Find two shoeboxes. One will be your soothing box. The other will be your worry box. Fill your soothing box with objects that make you feel happy and calm. They could be favorite toys, photos, and anything else that is important to you. You can even write calming words on paper and put them in this box, such as "happy," or the name of your pet or best friend.

2. Each time you feel uncertain, write your emotions on a small piece of paper. Put the paper in the worry box and take a deep breath. This box will hold your worries so you don't have to carry them in your head.

3. Then open your soothing box and choose an object. Think about why it matters to you. Spend a few minutes concentrating on that object. Do you feel calmer?

GLOSSARY

anxious
Worried or very eager
to do something.

cope
To deal with something effectively.

emotions
Feelings, such as happiness,
sadness, or anger.

energy
The ability or strength to do
things without getting tired.

focus
To concentrate on something.

meditate
To think deeply and quietly as a way
of relaxing your mind and body.

panic
To feel sudden, overwhelming
fear or anxiety.

reassures
Makes someone feel calm
and confident and gives the
person courage.

resolved
Found a solution to a problem
or settled a difficulty.

social anxiety
A strong and constant fear of being
watched and judged by others.

support
To give help, comfort,
or encouragement to
someone or something.

tense
Stretched stiff and tight, or unable
to relax.

TO LEARN MORE

FACT SURFER

Finding more information is as easy as 1, 2, 3.

1. Go to www.factsurfer.com

2. Enter "**facinguncertainty**" into the search box.

3. Choose your book to see a list of websites.

INDEX

Blue Owl Books are published by Jump!, 5357 Penn Avenue South, Minneapolis, MN 55419, www.jumplibrary.com

Copyright © 2023 Jump! International copyright reserved in all countries. No part of this book may be reproduced in any form without written permission from the publisher.

Library of Congress Cataloging-in-Publication Data

Names: Golkar, Golriz, author.
Title: Facing uncertainty / by Golriz Golkar.
Description: Minneapolis, MN: Jump!, Inc., [2023] | Series: Facing life's challenges | Includes index. | Audience: Ages 7–10
Identifiers: LCCN 2021059800 (print)
LCCN 2021059801 (ebook)
ISBN 9781636908168 (hardcover)
ISBN 9781636908175 (paperback)
ISBN 9781636908182 (ebook)
Subjects: LCSH: Uncertainty–Juvenile literature. | Anxiety in children–Juvenile literature.
Classification: LCC BF463.U5 G65 2023 (print)
LCC BF463.U5 (ebook) | DDC 155.4/1246–dc23/eng/20220111
LC record available at https://lccn.loc.gov/2021059800
LC ebook record available at https://lccn.loc.gov/2021059801

Editor: Eliza Leahy
Designer: Molly Ballanger

Photo Credits: Bangkok Click Studio/Shutterstock, cover (left); rangizzz/Shutterstock, cover (right); Shutterstock, 1; Kamira/Shutterstock, 3; Sriya Pixels/Shutterstock, 4 (left); LightField Studios/Shutterstock, 4 (right); Juice Verve/Shutterstock, 5 (background); kungverylucky/Shutterstock, 5 (foreground); Andrey_Popov/Shutterstock, 6–7; Cavan Images/Getty, 8; FG Trade/iStock, 9; Prostock-studio/Shutterstock, 10–11, 14–15; Serhii Bobyk/Shutterstock, 12–13; gradyreese/iStock, 16; Jose Luis Pelaez Inc/Getty, 17; Maskot/Getty, 18–19; AJ_Watt/iStock, 20–21.

Printed in the United States of America at Corporate Graphics in North Mankato, Minnesota.